DID YOU KNOW?
WHALES ARE A LOT LIKE YOU

M. R. Kaye

Copyright 2013 by M.R. Kaye
All Rights
Reserved Kindle
Edition

Due To The Sheer Size, and also that many whales are NOW endangered we have done our best to find quality images of the whales in the book. Some can only be taken from above so they may be obscured by waves.

Updated December 2018

TABLE OF CONTENTS

AREN'T THEY FISH?

I Thought Whales Were Fish, Since They Live In Water
Whales are a very special group of animals that spend their entire lives in the water. You will learn in this book what makes them special. One of the things that makes whales special is that they are much more like humans than they are like a fish.

For a long time, many people thought that whales were "just a type of fish" but now we know this is not true at all.

Whales are animals that live in the water, and they are very social, creatures who enjoy being together. They have a lot in common with you and me, including the special things that make them mammals!

WHAT IS A MAMMAL?

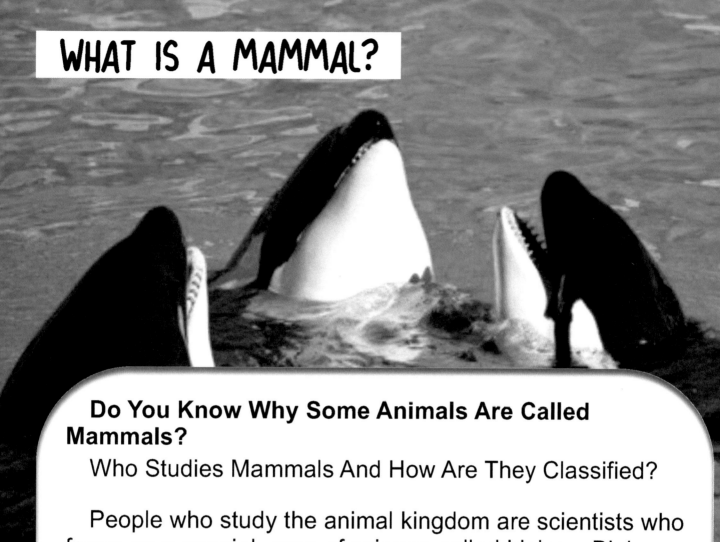

Do You Know Why Some Animals Are Called Mammals?

Who Studies Mammals And How Are They Classified?

People who study the animal kingdom are scientists who focus on a special area of science called biology. Biology is the study of living things, and biologists study living things. Zoology is the study of animals. Zoologists are biologists who study animals.

Did you know that scientists have a special way of grouping the animals that they study?

This way of grouping animals together is based on how alike or different living things are. A man named Carolus Linnaeus first grouped animals together this way long time ago. He lived in Sweden from 1707-1778 and made a special way to group and name over 4000 types of animals, including mammals.

The method of grouping living things together for science is really neat, and so is learning about how Dr. Linnaeus used it.

It would be fun to learn more about it on line. You could also try and see if you can use it to classify your favorite animal when you have time.

We won't have room here to learn about the ways a certain type of animal is separated into different groups by scientists. You can find more information about it online if you are interested.

Learn More Here: http://bit.ly/CarolusLinnaeus

You do need to know that how an animal is grouped is an important part of what makes an animal a mammal or not, at least by name.

All animals on the planet are in one really really big group, or kingdom called

Animalia. Animals that have a backbone like humans and whales, get put into a smaller group called Chordata. Then they are put into an even smaller group called Mammalia.Being in the Mammalia group makes an animal a mammal, but that is kind of a hard way to remember it, right? I mean, what exactly makes a scientist put an animal into the mammal group?

Here is a more basic way to think about the things that make an animal a mammal.

1. They have lungs and breathe air.
2. They have hair of some kind on their bodies.
3. They have milk producing glands in their bodies which females use to feed their young.
4. They give birth to live babies instead of laying eggs, for the most part, there
   are a few exceptions.
5. Their body temperature does not change with their environment, it stays consistent.

Don't forget the five things every mammal must have in common! Can you see that both humans and whales are mammals? What are some other animals that are mammals?

MORE WAYS WHALES ARE LIKE US

How Else Are Whales Similar To Humans?

Very Similar, Very Different Whales as a group are very similar. They also have a lot of differences between the different types we talked about here. This is called diversity. These differences are things like skin color, where they live, what they like to eat.

Humans have a lot of differences between them too. How many differences can you think of between you and your best friend?

Kings Of Their Ecosystem

Whales and humans both have no natural predators, or animals that are bigger or stronger than them which hunt them for food. This is true in the places where they live. Actually, humans sometimes cause problems for whales due to their actions, like polluting the ocean or killing whales for meat.

Culture

Whales and humans both have a lot of types of cultures, or things that bond a group together. Your culture is defined by where you come from and the things that you learned to do from a very young age. Lots of things impact culture. We are all human beings, but there are many cultures in our world. Whales have a similar experience of culture. Each group of whales does things a bit differently.

Language

Humans use language to express themselves, just as whales do. Each type or group of whales has their own unique language and can recognize the language of other groups.

Emotion and Affection

Whales, like humans are also very emotional and affectionate animals. They experience happiness, sadness, and love when positive things happen in their life. They feel fear, and can be very sad for a very long time after one of their friends or family members dies.

Aging

Female whales reach an age, much like female humans where their bodies make it impossible for them to have any more children. This is called Menopause.

WHALES BREATHE AIR

Humans can hold their breath under water for a very short period of time without using something to help them. How long can you hold your breath?

Whales can hold their breath for a very long time, but they don't have gills like fish do, so they cannot stay underwater forever. To stay alive, they have to come to the surface every day to take a breath. When they let the air out of their lungs through their blow hole, some water goes with it too.

That is what causes the spray of water, or spout that whales are so well known for.

WHALES HAVE HAIR

Humans, monkeys and gorillas are all covered in hair all over their bodies.

Whale hair is different from ours and is not always all over their bodies. They do have patches of thick, bristles. Sometimes, those bristles are even on their heads!

WHALES FEED THEIR BABIES MILK

Whales Make Milk To Feed Their Babies

Whales and humans both give birth to live babies. Most mamals give birth but a very few even lay eggs. We don't really have space to talk about the special mammals that lay eggs, here but there are three of them, see if you can find out what they are! We will cover them in another book.

Female Mammals, have special glands, called mammary glands. These glands make milk so that babies will have a food supply available to them from the moment they are born.

Human mammary glands are on the chest. Whale mammary glands are on the lower part of their bodies.

WHALES ARE WARM BLOODED

Whales Are Warm Blooded And Have A Consistent Body Temperature.

Whales and other mammals are warm blooded, which means that their bodies work from the inside out to keep or maintain a certain core body temperature no matter what the temperature around them is.

Cold blooded animals like frogs take on the temperature of whatever is around them. A whale also has a thick layer of fat under their skin to help protect them from the cold water that they live in.

A whale's perfect body temperature is 96 degrees. Our perfect body temperature is 98.6 degrees.

Have you learned to measure temperature yet?

Can you tell me how much difference there is between the whale's perfect body temperature and ours?

TYPES OF WHALES

Types Of Whales

Remember when we talked about how scientists have a way of grouping things together based on how alike or different they are? This is important when we talk about the types of whales there are too.

Did you know that there are over 86 different types or species of whale?

Some whales belong to the Baleen whale group, and others belong to the Toothed whale group. There are many species of whales that you should take the time to learn about. Here is a short list:

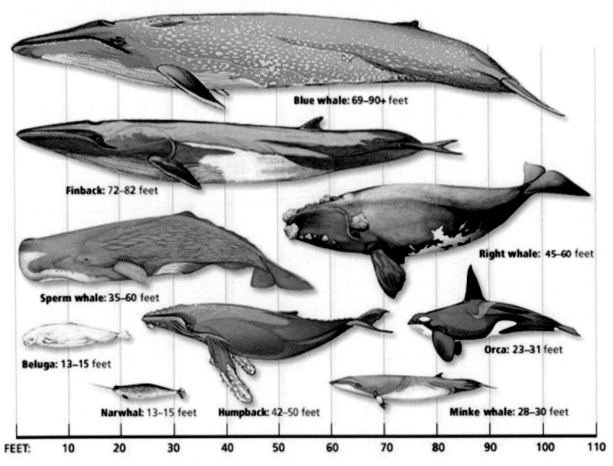

Blue whale: 69–90+ feet

Finback: 72–82 feet

Right whale: 45–60 feet

Sperm whale: 35–60 feet

Orca: 23–31 feet

Beluga: 13–15 feet

Narwhal: 13–15 feet

Humpback: 42–50 feet

Minke whale: 28–30 feet

FEET: 10 20 30 40 50 60 70 80 90 100 110

Read More : http://bit.ly/TypesOfWhales

Image attribution: Ocean.si.edu

TYPES OF BALEEN WHALES

Baleen Whales

Baleen whales have plates in their mouths made of the same material that our hair and fingernails are made out of, this is called keratin. These plates are sometimes called whalebone, and they grow all the time, just like our hair and nails too.

The plates help the whales that have them, filter the things that they eat out of the sea water that passes through their mouth. These whales eat things like plankton and small fish.

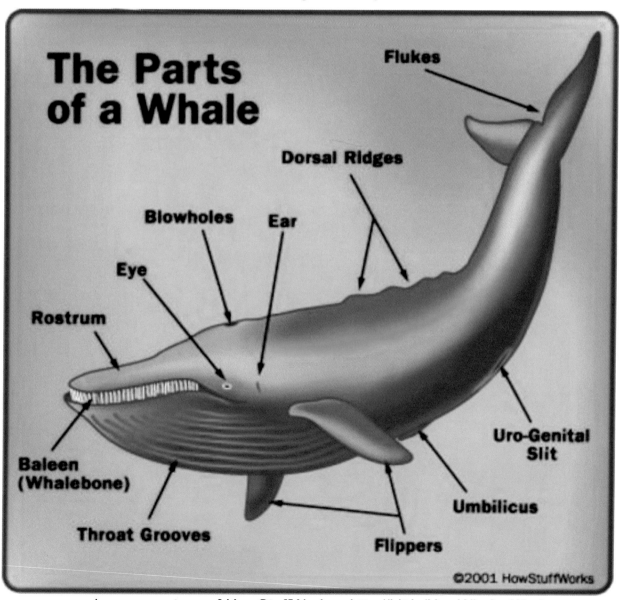

Image courtesy of HowStuffWorks - http://bit.ly/HowWhalesWork

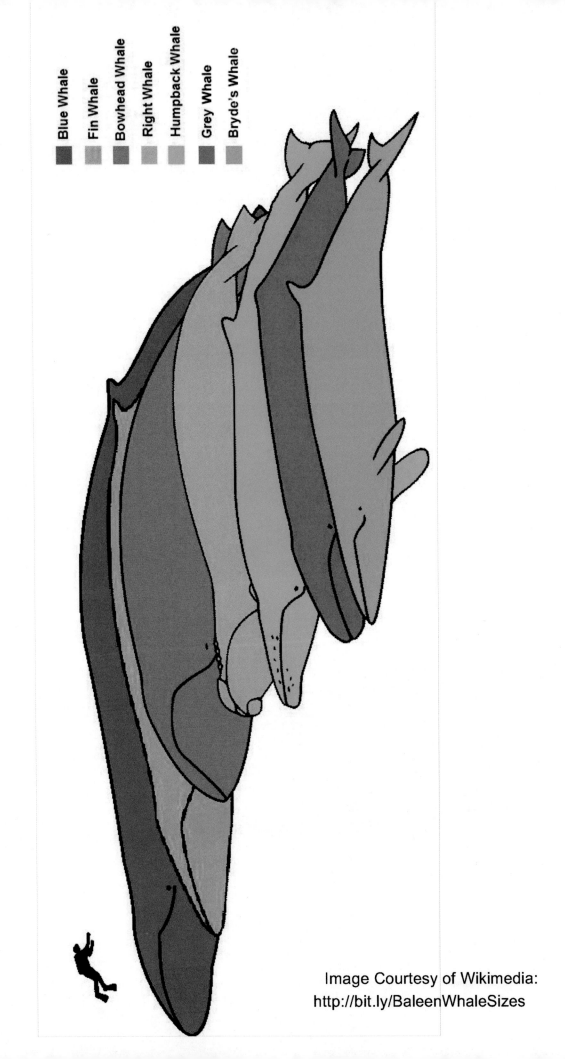

Blue Whale
Fin Whale
Bowhead Whale
Right Whale
Humpback Whale
Grey Whale
Bryde's Whale

Image Courtesy of Wikimedia:
http://bit.ly/BaleenWhaleSizes

BLUE WHALE

Blue Whale – Blue whales are the largest animal in the animal kingdom. They have skin that is blue or gray and sometimes they have spots!

Did you know that they can grow to be as long as 100 feet, often weigh nearly ***200 tons!***

Do you know how much a ton is?

One ton equals 2000 pounds!

FIN WHALE

Fin Whale – Fin whales are almost as large as Blue whales, and are larger than any dinosaur that ever lived. Their size does not mean they are slow.

They are actually quite fast, and earned the nickname "The Greyhounds of the Sea."

These whales have special kinds of fins that allow them to move quickly, and have a white spot on the right side of their face.

HUMPBACK WHALE

Humpback Whale –The Humpback whale, like the Gray whale is also a smaller sized type of whale. They do have very distinctive, long fins called dorsal fins. These fins have often been mistaken for wings. These whales also will go a long time without eating during the winter.

There are 10 more species of Baleen whale, hopefully now you want to learn about the others!

Wikipedia is one of our most favorite sites for learning about things. You can go here to learn more about Baleen Whales. https://en.wikipedia.org/wiki/Baleen_whale

GRAY WHALE

Gray Whale – The Gray whale is smaller than some of the others. The have gray spotted skin and can grow to be about 45 feet long. They might weigh 40 tons. There are two groups of these whales, one can be seen regularly off the coasts of the Western United States, and the other can be found off the coast of Asia. Can you find Asia on a map?

BALEEN WHALE VS TOOTHED WHALE COMPARISON CHART

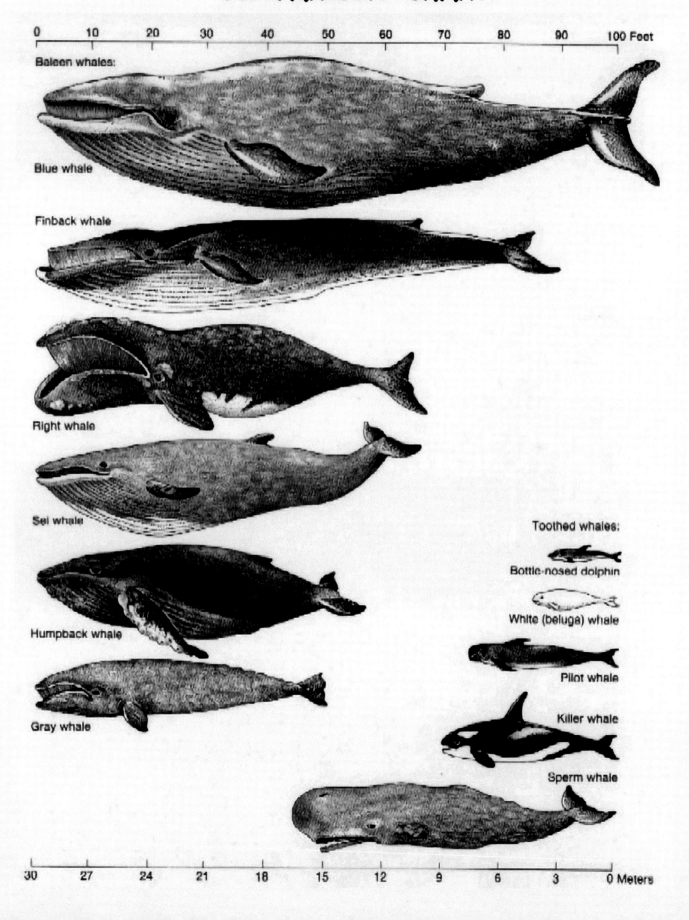

0   10   20   30   40   50   60   70   80   90   100 Feet

Baleen whales:

Blue whale

Finback whale

Right whale

Sei whale

Humpback whale

Gray whale

Toothed whales:

Bottle-nosed dolphin

White (beluga) whale

Pilot whale

Killer whale

Sperm whale

30   27   24   21   18   15   12   9   6   3   0 Meters

TYPES OF TOOTHED WHALES

Toothed whales have, teeth unlike the Baleen whales we just learned about. The number of teeth that they have depends on the type of whale, and there are a lot more whale types in this group than in the other! Toothed whales are also highly social, and form family groups called pods.

They use the melon, or fluid filled area between their forehead and nose for echolocation, or the way that they navigate and communicate. You may know about another creature that uses echolocation to get around. It is Bats.

There are 72 species of Toothed Whale
You can learn all about them here:
https://en.wikipedia.org/wiki/Toothed_whale

SPERM WHALE

Sperm whales are the biggest kind of toothed whale. They usually eat squid and can dive for up to 2 hours.

They can have anywhere from 17-30 pairs of teeth, weigh as much as 125,000 pounds, and can be as long as 60 feet.

NARWHAL

Narwhals are a medium sized toothed whale and the strangest looking of all of them. They live all year round up in the Arctic ocean so they do not travel, or migrate like some other whales do. The do not have a dorsal fin on their back.

You can tell a Narwhal whale by the very long straight tooth or tusk that the males will group. Did you know that this is actually a very, very long upper left Canine tooth?

You have canine teeth as well, they are the sharp pointed teeth you have in the front of your mouth. Can you imagine what you would look like if you had a tooth like that?

Do you know what a Unicorn is?

It is said that a long time ago in history that Narwhal sightings started the unicorn legends. Hundreds of years ago, people that found narwhal tusks that washed ashore thought they were from the mythical unicorn.

BELUGA WHALE

Beluga whales are also found in very cold, or arctic waters. They can grow to be 16 feet long, and weigh up to nearly 4,000 pounds. They have white skin, and do not have a fin on their back because they spend so much time under the ice, a fin would just rub on the ice.

They remain in icy waters just like the Narwhal does. Did you know they are called the sea canary? They were given this name because they create a very high pitched noise.

These are very social whales. They will gather in groups of up to 10 and in the summer, you can find groups of even hundreds or thousands.

KILLER WHALE

The Killer whale is also called the Orca. These are some of the mostly widely known of the whales.

It is a very smart animal that will form packs with others in its pod, and will hunt other whales or seals. Shamu at Sea World is a great example of an Orca.

Sometimes, these whales have protected humans in waters where there are lots of sharks.

Did you know that Orca's are called Killer Whales yet they are actually Dolphins? Scientists classify them as dolphins.

They are considered the largest dolphins in their class. This is confusing because Dolphins belong to the whale family..but of course not all whales are dolphins.

DOLPHINS AND PORPOISES?

What About Dolphins And Porpoises?

Did you know that Dolphins, porpoises and whales are all mammals like we are? We didn't really cover them too much by themselves in this book, but did you know that dolphins and porpoises are mammals like whales too?

Dolphins live in the ocean with whales, and eat many of the same things.

They also have very similar social groups, use echolocation (like bats do, to explore their environment) and have even more ways that they are alike.

There are also some big differences. Dolphins are smaller, faster swimmers and they come much closer to shore than the types of whales we talked about are willing or able to unless something is wrong with them.

Enjoy reading more about dolphins when you get done with this book. Look for our series on Dolphins and Porpoises. You can get It here https://amzn.to/2E7yRqJ

Looking at this next picture, what things do you think help you tell the difference between Dolphins and whales?

   Did you know that there are actually six species in the Dolphin family that are called "whales" but really are dolphins:

1. Killer Whale (Orca)
2. False Killer Whale
3. Pygmy Killer Whale
4. Melon-headed Whale
5. Short-finned Pilot Whale
6. Long-finned Pilot Whale

PROTECTING OUR WHALE FRIENDS

Sadly today Whales are in trouble in our oceans. Here are a few websites you may want to look at to learn more about how you can help whales, and learn more about these amazing creatures.

What project would you think you can do to help Whales? Maybe you can get your family and friends and even your community to help you. It is fun when people work together to help each other. Whales are a lot like you, after all.

This page from One Green Planet has information about the top organizations that are helping marine life today.

Find out more about how you can help our whale friends
http://bit.ly/ProtectWhales

ENDNOTES

Thank you so much for spending time with us today.
If you enjoyed this animal book, would you please take a minute to leave a review on Amazon? Even just a couple of sentences would be great. When you leave a review, it helps others find my books for their children.
Thank You,
M. R Kaye
Find All My Books Here https://amzn.to/2PrN97r

and in other fine book stores

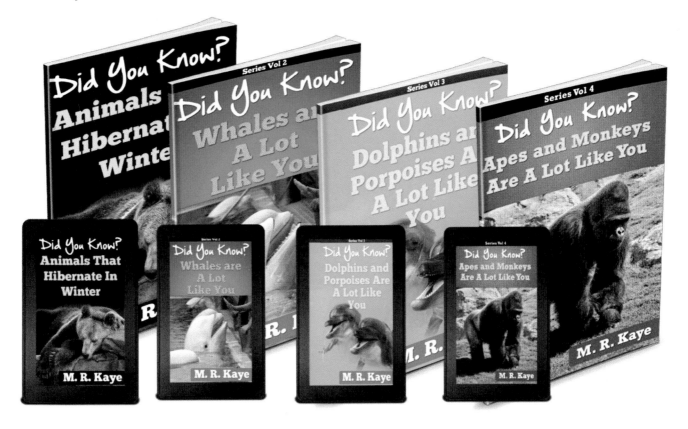